CW00536383

1

Bonsai
The Beginner's Guide

Bonsai

The Beginner's Guide to Cultivate, Grow, Shape, and Show Off Your Bonsai Tree

Includes History, Styles of Bonsai, Types of Bonsai Trees, Trimming, Wiring, Repotting, and Watering

Masao Hideyoshi

Copyright © 2017 by Masao Hideyoshi

All rights reserved. No part of this publication may be reproduced, distributed, or transmitted in any form or by any means, including photocopying, recording, or other electronic or mechanical methods, without the prior written permission of the publisher, except in the case of brief quotations embodied in critical reviews and certain other noncommercial uses permitted by copyright law.

CAC Publishing
ISBN: 978-1-948489-01-0

Masao Hideyoshi

Table of Contents

Introduction 8

History 12

Bonsai Tree Styles 17

    The Formal Upright 19

    The Informal Upright 21

    The Slanting Style 23

    The Cascade (Waterfall) Style 25

    Semi Cascade (Waterfall) Style 27

Types of Trees 29

    Beech Trees 29

    Cedar 29

    Cherry 30

    Elm 30

    Gingko 31

    Camellia 32

    Cedar Elm 33

    Chinese Elm 33

    Dwarf Pomegranate 34

    Ficus 34

    Japanese Black Pine 35

    Seeds or Saplings? 36

    Nursey Stock 37

Planting 41

    Inside or Outside 41

Pruning and Trimming 47

    Tools 47

    How to Prune or Trim 48

Wiring 53

    Best Time to Wire 57

Water and Fertilizer 61

Repotting 63

Seasonal 67

Showing Off Your Bonsai 71

Introduction

"Bonsai art is the display of a landscape - without the landscape." --Nobu Kajiwara

This quote couldn't be truer. Raising and shaping bonsai trees can be a relaxing and enjoyable hobby. It is, however, a hobby that requires a lot of patience. When you take a sapling and shape it as you please, you'll be creating your very own piece of living art!

The term bonsai translates to tray planting or plant in a pot. Bonsai, however, is so much more than simply planting in a pot. The objective of bonsai is to design the illusion of vast size and age. This is done by designing a bonsai with hardy roots that stretch out in all directions, which shows a sense of stability, a wide trunk that thins out as it reaches upward, a clear apex, and well-placed, shaped and trimmed branches. This appearance all comes together in a unique blend of symmetry and proportion. It also must be displayed in a pot which compliments the plant material.

Bonsai is the art of growing trees in a small space to recreate certain environmental conditions like vast age, extreme weathering, gnarled and bent form, landscape, or other factors. Bonsai trees are inspired by conditions created in nature. The point of bonsai is to simulate some of nature's most breath taking and awe-inspiring effects on trees in a smaller scale.

When first taking up bonsai, you are at the start of an experience that will grow your horizons in a multitude of ways. You might even find a new sense of appreciation of nature; you will begin looking at trees, bushes and even shrubs differently than you ever have before. You will probably even find yourself looking around all the worst parts of the local nurseries where they store the plants that are mostly unwanted. The ways in which the art of bonsai might change you is as variable as nature itself, but one thing is for certain: Bonsai will change the way that you view nearly everything.

For the Japanese, there is a tie to several of the principles that their society is founded on. Zen Buddhism - where the pastime began, man, nature, elements and revision all are interlaced into this technique of meditation and expression. To our world now, bonsai is seen as a specialty that allows a larger comprehension of, and being with, nature; and additionally, as a way to beautify our gardens.

The tree and the pot used with bonsai create one melodic entity in which the shape, essence and shade of each compliments the other. It is not sufficient to plant a tree in a pot and then leave the rest to nature. The tree must be shaped.

Each branch must be trimmed or eliminated until the desired image is reached. From then on, that image is either maintained or improved by a constant routine of trimming and shaping.

Bonsai is the art of dwarfing plants or trees and growing them into a visually appealing shape by growing, pruning and training the trees into containers according to certain means.

Overall, bonsai is a fun and interesting pastime or even profession to undertake. Certain famous theologians have stated that bonsai is 90% art and only a mere 10% of horticulture, it must also be said that a flourishing bonsai is definitely a masterpiece of horticulture.

Upon its arrival in the Western world, this fun and enjoyable pastime has never turned back, and has grown a substantial range of plant materials and creative techniques.

With enough care, bonsai can live for centuries, with some specimens even being passed from one generation to the next, admired for their age, and revered as a present-day reminder of those who have cared for them in years past. Although these bonsai are an amazing thing of beauty – so carefully nourished over the years and holding such a vast amount of knowledge, age is not required for success. It is far more important that the tree possess the artistic effect wanted, that it be in correct proportion to the pot, and that it is healthy.

Bonsai is a dramatic reflection of a natural tree. It is a likeness, an illusion of nature. It is an artful deception that defies the senses. The best bonsai are illusionists' tricks that have deceived the eye into seeing a magical land or a faraway place. We all must try to become the illusionist.

In this book, we will teach you various bonsai techniques and how to grow an artistic, living masterpiece of your own. The best thing about bonsai is that there isn't any right or wrong way to do it. We can offer many tips and tricks to create your own bonsai, but how you choose to do it is ultimately up to you. Enter the beautiful world of bonsai and you will surely gain a new insight into life.

History

The history of bonsai is lengthy and illustrious. China is where Bonsai appeared first a millennium ago. The Chinese were the first to grow trees in pots. These first types had little foliage and rough, twisted trunks which often looked like dragons, animals and birds. There are a multitude of myths and stories about Chinese bonsai. The deformed or animal-like trunks and root patterns are still treasured today.

With Japan's embracement of many cultural trademarks of China - bonsai was also adopted during the Kamakura period (1185 - 1333) by way of Zen Buddhism - which at that time was quickly spreading through Asia. The exact time is arguable, but it is probable that it began in 1195 AD since there seems to be a mention of it in a scroll from that time period.

When bonsai was adopted by Japan, the art was cultivated to a degree not yet begun in China. Eventually, the trees were not only kept by the Buddhist monks in their monasteries. They were popularized by the aristocracy as a symbol of status and distinction. The principles and ideology of bonsai were largely revised over the years. For the Japanese, bonsai epitomizes a blend of firm ancient beliefs with the Eastern principles of the relationship between man, soul and nature.

Whether this was meant to be a positive statement or not, it leads us to think that raising dwarfed and gnarled trees in pots was a common practice among the upper class of Japan by the Kamakura period. In the 14th century, bonsai was seen as a highly refined art form, so it would have been an established practice for years before that time.

Bonsai were brought inside and put on display at times by the Japanese elite. Bonsai became a meaningful part of Japanese life by being showcased on shelves that were designed specifically for this purpose. These elaborate plants were no longer banished to outdoor display, but the techniques of training and pruning did not evolve until later. The trees were still being taken from the wild at this time.

Bonsai grew to a much more advanced understanding and enhancement, but the pots that were implemented were deeper than what is used nowadays. The chief point in shaping bonsai was the removal of all but the most necessary parts of the tree. The elimination of everything that wasn't essential was symbolic of the Japanese ideology of this time.

Near this time, bonsai came to be more commonplace with the general Japanese public. This increased demand for the little trees that had been gathered from the wild and began the art form within the society and traditions of the country.

Eventually, bonsai began to take on various styles, and each differed greatly from one another. Bonsai artists eventually began introducing other culturally significant components in their bonsai plantings such as stones, additional plants, little buildings and people.

This art is called *bon-kei*. They began to recreate on a smaller scale the landscapes seen in nature. This was called *sai-kei* which further increased the diverse range of possibilities for bonsai.

Eventually, at about the mid-19th century, after more than 230 years of global isolation, Japan opened to the rest of the world. Word spread from those who had visited Japan of the little trees in ceramic pots which mimicked aged, gnarled, towering trees in nature. Additional exhibitions in London, Vienna and Paris in the later part of the century, and particularly the Paris World Exhibition in the year 1900, opened the eyes of the world to the art of bonsai.

Because of this increased demand for bonsai, the now quickly growing industry had an insufficiency of naturally occurring, dwarfish plants which led to the commercial growth of bonsai by artists through forcing young plants to grow to look like bonsai. Many basic styles were utilized, and artists used various materials such as bamboo skewers, wire, and growing techniques to accomplish this, which in turn further advanced this art. The Japanese began to take advantage of the increased interest in this art form by opening nurseries that were dedicated to the sole purpose of growing, training and exporting these popular bonsai trees.

An assortment of plants are now being utilized to cater to worldwide climates and to create neater foliage and more befitting growth habits. Bonsai techniques like raising trees from seeds or from cuttings and the styling and grafting of unique or tender material onto strong root stock were further advanced.

Bonsai has since evolved to show changing tastes and preferences in the great variety of countries, societies and conditions in which it is now practiced.

In Japan, bonsai are still viewed as an emblem of their culture and ideals. The days of Bonsai being reserved for the noble are long gone. It is now a hobby appreciated by managerial and shop workers alike.

The Japanese mainly focus on utilizing native plants for their bonsai, such as pines, azaleas, and maples. These are considered the traditional bonsai plants. In other countries however, people are more open to other options.

The evolution of bonsai over the last 200 years is truly incredible. It may be a symbol of how small the world is, as people from Europe to the United States and even Greenland have taken up bonsai as a hobby.

Bonsai Tree Styles

Remember, as a beginner, no particular bonsai style is the correct or incorrect style. Bonsai is intended to be a portrayal of a tree in nature. Creating a bonsai masterpiece is commensurate to how you view that tree. You are not a student of a bonsai master, you are merely being given direction on how to design your own bonsai. What you make of it is up to your own imagination.

Your goal should be to make your bonsai trees look as natural as you can. Allow the tree to suggest its own possibilities. If the trunk bends to the left, allow it to bend in that direction. Make it a feature of your bonsai. Allow the tree to show you what it is meant to be. Hear what it is telling you. Then you will create something beautiful!

Bonsais should appear to be old even when they are young. You should try to project the look of great age in your tree in a miniature form. Even a young tree can be groomed to appear as if it has been growing for decades.

Two components that give the illusion of age to trees are the size of the trunk and the degree to which it tapers. The trunks of bonsai (in most styles) should be thick at the base and taper smoothly towards the top.

There are two general kinds of bonsai: the classic and the informal. In the first, the trunk is thicker at the base and tapers steadily towards the top; it is the opposite of the 'bunjin' of informal, a style that is much tougher to master.

When you first begin a bonsai, you should always remember that you are working with a living plant. Study its natural characteristics and you might visualize in them a befitting style. Sometimes you can train a plant into multiple styles, even if it is straight like a beech or delicately thin like a maple. If one style suits a particular plant, you can still change this in many ways.

Most importantly you should never try to force a bonsai to grow in a style it is not accustomed to. Observe the natural growth patterns of the plant you are attempting to grow and build on the pattern given to it by nature.

The following are the five main bonsai styles:

The Formal Upright

The formal upright occurs when it has been grown in the open under optimal conditions. The most critical factor for this style is that the trunk be very straight, tapering naturally and evenly from bottom to top. The branches must be spaced symmetrically so that they appear well balanced when seen from any direction. It is a difficult style to achieve. The best trees for formal upright style are Juniper, pine, and spruce.

To create an effective formal upright style, make certain that approximately a third of the trunk is visible from the front. This can be from the bottom to the first branch or cumulatively, as viewed through the tracery of its branches.

Usually, the placement of branches should follow a pattern. The first branch up from the base should be the longest and in proportion generally is trained to grow to an equivalent of a third of the height of the tree. This should be the heaviest branch and should come close to making a right angle to the trunk of the tree.

The second branch should directly oppose the first branch and should be higher on the trunk. As the branches go higher, they should taper into a cone-like shape.

The top of the bonsai should be thick with foliage. It should be very full and it should be difficult to see its internal structure through the foliage

The tip of this formal upright bonsai should have a slight forward curve, to appear to be leaning toward the viewer. Depending on which type of tree you utilize, the entire tree doesn't *have* to be symmetrical, but the branches may ascend by alternating on each side.

The branches and trunk of the formal upright bonsai should have a distinctive taper. This is achieved by trimming off the tip of the trunk or branch with each new year and wiring a new branch into place to create the apex. This is difficult to accomplish, but it produces an incredible result when the trunk begins to mature and the taper becomes more obvious.

The Informal Upright

These trees will bend away from wind and shade, and towards the sun. The informal upright bonsai will have a trunk that is bent to the right or left. It should not be bent towards the observer. This applies to every type of bonsai. The trunk and branches should not be leaning towards the observer when the bonsai is seen from the front.

The best trees to use for informal upright style are the Japanese maple, Trident maple, or most any conifer or other ornamental tree.   A pomegranate or other flowering tree will create a beautiful result.

The informal upright bonsai uses the same basic ideas of the formal upright bonsai. The style still has a tapered trunk, but the trunk direction and branch placement is more natural and closely mimics the way a tree would look in nature when exposed to the wind and sun at a young age. The trunk takes on curves or twists and the branches are placed to balance this effect.

Like the formal upright, the top of the tree is heavy with full foliage and despite the informal trunk, should be located directly above the base. This is a quality of this style.

The Slanting Style

Trees that slant occur because of winds and shade during early growth. Whether it is curved or straight, the whole trunk will lean at a definite angle. The sturdier roots will grow out away from the slant of the trunk, to support its weight.

Many classes of tree will work with this style. This style is similar to the informal upright as the trunk may be curved or straight, but it must be on an angle. It doesn't matter if it is a left or right angle, but it must never be towards the front and the apex should *not* be directly over the base.

This is a simple style that can be created with various methods. At a young age, the bonsai tree can be trained to grow at a slant by wiring until it reaches the required position. The tree can also be forced to grow at a slant by placing the pot on a slant, forcing the tree to grow in a different manner.

Another similarity shared by formal, informal and slanted styles is the number three. The lowermost branches of these styles are always grouped in sets of three, and this grouping should start a third of the way up the trunk. The lowest three branches almost surround the trunk, with two branches reaching forward, one above the other. The third branch, coming from a point amid the first two branches, is grown at an angle to make the greenery appear lower than the first two.

This arrangement offers a simple way to tell front from back and sets the tone of the whole layout.

The Cascade (Waterfall) Style

The flourishing top of this bonsai stretches below the base of the container. The trunk has a normal taper and gives the delusion of fighting against the forces of gravity. The beautiful branches seem to be reaching to the light. The twisting trunk brings to mind reminiscent a winding stream making its way down a mountain.

There are several kinds of trees that can be utilized to create a cascading bonsai. The major point is to make sure the tree isn't naturally straight. It is difficult to force a straight trunk into a cascading bonsai.

When done properly, this bonsai can be particularly beautiful. The trunk grows down lower than the pot and creates the illusion that the tree is being held down gravitationally. The trunk usually twists as if to imitate a flowing stream with graceful alternating branches extending from it.

All you need to create this style is a tall, slim pot which will complement the style and permit for the waterfall, and the sort of plant that will effortlessly adopt this style if trained correctly.

You can wire the core trunk to hang beneath the edge of the pot, with the emphasis on the main. Attention should be given to keeping the branches even and level to the trunk. Another important point to keep in mind is that both waterfall and semi-waterfall must be placed dead center in the pot, which is the opposite of what to do for any other style.

Semi Cascade (Waterfall) Style

The top of a semi-cascade, like the cascade, extends over the edge of the pot, but doesn't reach below the base. The style would happen in nature when trees sprout on cliffs or near the edge of a body of water. The angle of the trunk is not perfect, but as long as the effect is mainly horizontal, even if the plant extends below the level of the pot rim. Any visible roots will balance the trunk.

Trees that work best with this style are flowering cherry, cedars, and junipers. Many people think this style of bonsai is the ultimate personification of beauty in the art.

Types of Trees

Almost any tree or shrub can be used for bonsai, however, Pines are difficult for beginners. It's best to choose a species that is easier to work with for your first try.

One tree that is great for beginners is the juniper. They are relatively cheap, can be trimmed and shaped during most seasons, and can be used to grow more trees.

Beech Trees

Beech trees also make excellent bonsai and are a favorite of many. They are best grown in informal style. Leaf trimming every other year will create smaller leaves on the larger styles. Leaf trimming should be done as early as you can because if beech is left too late it may not come back into leaf that year.

The Southern Beeches have both evergreen and deciduous species. They can be cared for the same way as beeches from the northern hemisphere, but you do not leaf trim the evergreens. They don't have special requirements, but thrive better in an alkaline (lime) soil than they will in a peat based compost.

Cedar

There are several species termed Cedar. When potted, cedars have weak root systems. Their fleshy roots are susceptible to damage by frost. In cold weather these trees must be sheltered. They grow best in a looser clumpy soil than their transitory counterparts.

Cherry

The Cherry tree is part of the biggest plant family on Earth called the Rosaceous. This family is quite diverse and includes apricot, plums, and peach trees, any of which can be used for bonsai.

The Apricot is the quickest to flower in this family and is known as the Mume in Japan.

All trees in the cherry family grow easily from seed, sown in the autumn. The seeds require the cold of winter to germinate. Whether they are grown from seed or cuttings it can still take over a decade for them to flower.

Pruning should be done in the summer, allowing enough time for next year's flower buds to develop.

These trees should not be allowed to grow fruit since it can stress the tree beyond its ability to survive.

Elm

The elm tree, with species in most of the northern hemisphere are easily obtained and can thrive in a range of soils. The two species you are most likely to find from suppliers are the Zelcova and Chinese Elm.

These are both excellent trees, but the Chinese elm is more susceptible to frost. Try whichever elm grows in your area since all elms make good bonsai.

The Chinese Elm is sometimes mistakenly sold as an indoor tree. It is an easy tree to grow. Deciduous in temperate areas, it can keep its leaves in tropical and sub-tropical areas. It can be grown from seed, but of course doing so would not produce quick results.

The seed germinates easily should you wish to try one, but cuttings and layering are the best ways to grow.

Elms respond well to leaf trimming, and on a vigorous tree this can be done 2 times in one season, but not every year.

Gingko

The Ginkgo Biloba (which is also known by the name Maidenhair tree), along with Larch, Swamp Cypress and Dawn Redwood is a conifer that drops its leaves over the winter. Until the 1940's, it was thought to be extinct and was known only from fossilized leaves until live specimens were found growing in China. This tree has a sex classification of male or female.

Ginkgo is good for Bonsai, but because of its growth patterns can be to be hard to style. The Ginko is best left to take on its own shape. This shape will usually be much like the flame on a candle. Ginko doesn't respond well to being trained with wire. Shaping should be done by pruning. It will need protection in the winter because of its soft roots. The leaves of this tree can be trimmed by pinching off with your fingers.

Camellia

Camellias are among the most beautiful of all bonsai due to their bountiful flowers. They stand up well to pruning in the winter or after they flower. They require partial shade and protection from frost in the winter. Camellias are best used for Informal upright style with single or multiple trunks, or Cascades in large sizes.

Cedar Elm

Cedar elms are an excellent choice for bonsai and like most elms, can survive some neglect. The rough, fissured bark is one of its most attractive features. Most specimens are collected from the wild and will almost always appear aged. The branches ramify easily with pinching of shoots and the leaves are not large. This is a good tree for beginners. They do well when kept on the dryer side since their natural environment is hot and dry. They can thrive in almost any type of soil. Like most trees, they use more water in the spring. They can be kept in full or dappled sunshine, but if they get too much they can turn yellowish and they will turn their leaves edge side up to limit the exposure of the leaves to the sun's rays.

Chinese Elm

The Chinese Elm tree can be used for inside or outside bonsai and are another good choice for beginners. They have a predictable growth pattern and don't require a perfect pruning technique.

Some varieties of Chinese Elm have smooth bark and others have a rougher, more cork-like appearance which cracks and becomes fissured as they age. This adds a depth of character to your bonsai. The smoother bark varieties are not as hardy as those with rough bark. These trees are quite versatile and can be kept in shade or in full sun, but care should be taken in hotter months to give it some shade so it doesn't dry out.

Dwarf Pomegranate

The dwarf pomegranate is quite popular with bonsai enthusiasts, mostly due to its flowers. The pomegranate produces beautiful brightly colored flowers. It also has a gnarled trunk that effortlessly takes on the aged appearance that is popular in bonsai. Its dark leaves are a deep green with metallic highlights. Not long after the first appearance of flowers, it will produce attractive, round, red pomegranates approximately the size of golf balls.

It can be used for several styles of bonsai. It will thrive in hot, sunny conditions, in places such as the Mediterranean.

Some people have a "fake" ficus tree in their home or office. These are the larger species. A miniature ficus can make a lovely bonsai addition.

Ficus

The Ficus, also known as a rainforest fig, is a plant which is well suited to bonsai. Figs are tropical plants found growing wild in south-east Asian jungles. There are several hundreds of species that make up this tree family.

The tiny flowers of this tree are totally enclosed in the developing fruits which occur in the leaf axils each year. As a bonsai, however, fruiting is not common. Figs will do best in full sun to part-shade. Humus-rich, slightly damp, but well drained soil and shelter from cold are a must.

Rainforest figs produce roots from the branches and the trunk. Whether to leave these on or remove them and bring them into the design is a controversial issue for some bonsai enthusiasts. At first the roots will be brittle, but eventually they strengthen when they reach nutrients. The aerial roots of the banyan fig are usually showcased in clasped to rocks style.

Japanese Black Pine

Japanese black pine is the embodiment of bonsai. Not many trees can carry the unflappable power or the subtle sophistication of bonsai to the degree that a black pine can. Black pine requires many years to reach the mature look of a superior specimen. Because of this, it's necessary that those who decide to grow them be steadfast in their care of the tree. Growing black pine for bonsai brings with it a responsibility to prepare and to maintain good material for future generations to work with.

Left on its own, a black pine would develop long branches that emerge in whorls from the trunk with foliage at the tips. The higher branches would be dominant and leave the lower branches weaker. It requires constant care and maintenance to stay in bonsai trim. Luckily black pine is a strong tree and responds well to bonsai techniques.

Of course, there are other varieties of trees that would work with bonsai. These suggestions just give you a starting point.

Seeds or Saplings?

Once you have your species chosen, it's time to think about your tree. You can start with a sapling or by planting a seed.

It takes a long time to grow a bonsai from a seed and while it may be nice to have total control over your bonsai from start to finish, it may not be feasible to begin with a seed unless of course you happen to begin your bonsai hobby when you are still a toddler!

Life is too short to wait for a seed to become a proper plant with a 1-2-centimeter trunk. So, unless you are considering doing a mini bonsai which are only about 4 inches tall, we advise against starting from a seed.

You can purchase a young sapling at your local nursery or any garden store. This way you will have more immediate results as you cultivate not only the tree but your artistic skills.

Trees used for bonsai are just ordinary tees or plants, they are not specialized hybrids. Any plant can be used, but small leaf varieties will work best no matter what size it would grow to if found in the wild.

When shopping at your local garden store or nursery, look for low-priced plants with thick trunks that you can turn into bonsai through the various methods we have discussed. You can even look around your own yard and see if anything appears to have good bonsai potential.

Only the quality of the tree matters, not whether you purchase it, or found it in your own backyard.

The experience and story of how you found or chose the bonsai will add historical and emotional value to the bonsai, which increases its value as a piece of art.

Choose a plant that will be able to accept the stress of being cut, wired, and replanted. Cotoneasters, Lonicera and Junipers are great starters for Shohin growing. You can find them in nurseries in suitable sizes for beginners.

Most importantly, you should choose a tree that can thrive in your climate and meet the requirements of good bonsai.

Nursey Stock

There are five things that you should be looking for when you are shopping at the nursery.

First, check the roots for the appearance of a strong foundation. The roots, at the base of the trunk, should be spread in a radial pattern (this will not be as visible on junipers) and should provide a sense of stability and draw your eye to the line of the tree, focusing your attention on the trunk.

Next look at the trunk. What you are looking for will depend on the style you want to create, but in most cases, you will be looking for a trunk with a wide base that gradually tapers towards the top. If you are planning a different style you will need to look for a tree with a trunk that curves in fascinating ways. Follow the main trunk to its highest point. Is it appealing to you? Can you see the possibility of the design you want in this plant?

Next, you should look at the branching outline. Seek out thick bottom branches with thinner branches towards the top. These branches will create the chief construction of your tree. Hopefully at this point a style will be suggesting itself. Can you see the beginnings of the style you want in this tree? What kind of shaping may be required in order for this to become the tree you envision? Do you see beauty in this mass of twigs that others may miss? How can you best make that beauty emerge?

Last, but not least, you should check that this plant is healthy. Pull it out of the container and check for white fibrous roots around the perimeter of the soil. This would suggest good health, as would colorful leaves and new growth. If there are no signs of good health choose another tree. Remember, you need a plant that can survive the process of potting and pruning.

The plant you choose should have attractive bark. The trunk should give the appearance of age. The trunk should be thick, but must be in proportion and should gradually thin towards the apex. One or two of the main branches might need to be shortened to highlight the vertical line of the trunk and give it a more balanced appearance.

To give the illusion of age, the upper third of the root structure of a mature bonsai is usually exposed. The branches should look proportioned. It should almost give the illusion that they are floating. You don't want too many branches crowded onto one side, or too many more on the bottom than you have on the top. When looking down at the bonsai from the top, check for unsightly gaps and flaws. The top branches should not over shadow the bottom branches.

Not all plants are suitable for bonsai. It's best if your tree has all parts in proportion. It should have small leaves or leaves that can be made small. Plants with large leaves will be out of proportion with the rest of your bonsai tree.

At last you have your tree. Next, we plant it!

Planting

Inside or Outside

Cultivating bonsai is usually considered an outdoor art. There are, however, options for indoor and outdoor bonsai.

One opinion is that trees are outdoor plants and just because they get planted in a pot does not suddenly make them indoor plants. Some people think that if you bring bonsai indoors, they will die. While this is not always true, outdoor plants are usually more successful than those grown indoors.

Trees require a lot of sunlight and care to grow. So, keep in mind that even when they are planted in a pot indoors instead of the ground they still have the same needs.

Bonsai are trees and even when grown indoors will require outdoor conditions. They need a lot of light, proper levels of humidity, air circulation, and many species require the cold winter temperatures to go dormant. When living inside homes, trees get much less light than they would outside. Our central heating systems cause the air to be dry which can also cause problems.

Certain species are better able to adapt to indoor living conditions than others. Some species are just not able to handle the cold of winter.

It is much easier to grow bonsai outdoors than inside. Outdoor species rarely die right away when grown indoors. Some can live many months to several years. These Bonsai gradually lose their health and become susceptible to bugs and disease. Sooner or later they will show signs of ill health such as yellowing of leaves and gradual death.

Varieties that are most likely to thrive indoors the aralia, azalea, ficus Norfolk pine, serissa, gardenia, and boxwood. All of these are woody-stemmed plants, which means they can have their limbs wired to direct the way you want them to grow.

Tropical and subtropical varieties cannot survive temperatures below 40 - 50 degrees Fahrenheit. These plants can only be left outdoors when temperatures are warmer. The light inside the house should be filtered sunlight from a south, east, or west window. Grow lights used for 12 hours per day will work well. If trees are put outside in summer, place them in partial shade.

The coniferous species make the most successful bonsai; however, they will not survive indoor cultivation for more than 3 years.

Temperate bonsai should be left outside all year long in mild climates. In cold climates, temperate climate trees should be left outside in the warm seasons, but will need protection when winter comes. It is possible to grow temperate climate trees inside during winter if they are given the required time of dormancy first.

It is best for beginners to start growing bonsai outdoors. Even though a few species can be grown inside all year-round if allowed a dormant period, this takes skills that are usually obtained after a few years of experience. It may be tempting for beginners to grow them inside, but if you are new to bonsai it is best started outside.

First, you will need an appropriate container. The bonsai with its pot and soil are independent of the ground, due to its roots not being planted in it. It remains a separate entity, but is still a great part of nature. Hence the expression heaven and earth in one container.

A bonsai tree should always be planted slightly off-center in its pot (unless cascade or semi-cascade). Not only is asymmetry a vital part of the visual effect, but the center is a symbol of the place where heaven and earth meet. Symbolically nothing else should take up this space.

Another symbolic necessity is a triangular pattern. Three virtues are required to create a bonsai: honesty, integrity and beauty. This trinity represents bonsai.

Because you will need to trim the roots, you will start with one container and use another later on for repotting. The first containers are training containers.

Select any container you like that is the appropriate size. There is a vast assortment of shapes, colors and sizes to choose from. They can be purchased from garden stores, nurseries or online retailers.

It is best to use a deep container for cascading plants. Tall trees that will end up planted in shallow containers should be started in shallow pots. All the drain holes in your training pots will need to be a minimum of a half inch in diameter.

Cascade and semi cascade styles look their best in round or rectangular containers. Plant them in the center of the container with the branches spilling over the sides. Upright trees should always be placed off center as previously discussed. They should be placed a third of the distance from the edge and look best in rectangular or oval containers.

The pot selected should complement the tree and not be overly large. The depth of the container should equal the girth of the trunk on your tree, though this is not a hard and fast rule that must be enforced.

Select a wide and shallow container so as not to detract the emphasis from the plant. A wide, flat container provides the sense of calm serenity one would find in the deep forest. Choose a pot whose length is about two-thirds the height of the tree.

If the tree is fatter than its height, use the width as your measure for the container size. Choose a planter with a width about two-thirds the height of the tree and a depth of about 1 1/2 times the trunk's diameter.

Choose colors that complement the tree, for example a brightly colored container for a flowering plant or for a deciduous tree that has brilliant autumn leaves. Choose a more muted color for a pine or cedar. If the bark of your tree has a rough texture, a bit of texture on the container complements it.

Keep in mind that the container is not permanent. Eventually you will have to re-pot it to prevent it from becoming root bound. We will discuss re-potting in a later chapter.

Once your bonsai has been potted you can add moss or other small plants around it to give the illusion of a full-sized tree in nature.

Now, let's consider the tools you will need to start your own bonsai masterpiece.

Pruning and Trimming

Tools

Bonsai do not require many tools and what you need can range in cost from a mere few dollars to hundreds of dollars. There is a wide range in both quality and cost of tools. Start with the best set of basic tools that fit your budget. With proper care they will last a long time.

The most important three tools are sharp scissors, concave cutters, and wire cutters.

The scissors must be sharp enough to trim the bonsai. You can start with small pruning shears, but it is best to purchase shears made especially for working with bonsai.

Concave cutters are used for cutting branches off the tree. They leave behind a concave wound that heals quicker than a straight cut. In time it leaves a callous that makes it hard to tell a cut was ever made.

Eventually you will need a good pair of wire cutters. Any time you put wire on, you will eventually need to cut it off. Wire cutters will let you cut the wire all the way to the bark of the tree without damaging it.

To train and position the branches it is best to use anodized copper wire. You should buy several thicknesses of this wire. It is quite flexible until you bend it. Once bent it will set and keep its position. Further detail is discussed later in the wiring chapter.

As you become more comfortable working with bonsai and gain some experience, there are additional tools that can help you do even more with your trees.

Knob cutters are much like the concave cutters mentioned earlier, but they have a round head. They will leave a small hollowed out scar in the tree.

A folding saw is capable of cutting through thicker branches than can be handled by knob or concave cutters. These are helpful if you are working on larger trees.

For detail work on smaller trees it is best to use small scissors. These are a must when working on a twiggy growth where it is difficult to get close enough with large shears.

A root rake will be needed to gently clean away the dirt from a root ball before repotting a tree.

Last but not least, tweezers can be extremely helpful when grooming bonsai. They can be used to pinch back new growth, and to remove unwanted objects. Bonsai tweezers usually are equipped with a small trowel on the end for patting down moss and for sowing your seeds.

How to Prune or Trim

A lot of pruning will likely be needed when starting with a tree from a nursery. You should remove any excess of foliage and undesirable limbs. All cuts should be made above a bud, a side branch, or a main fork in your tree. All buds should be removed except for those on the outside of the trunk. This will force growth upward and outward. Stubs should be left flush with the stems. Be careful not to cut back so much that the main branches are weakened.

Don't shear a bonsai like you would with hedges. The goal is to make your plant look like a mature tree. Keep the branches growing towards open areas and away from each other. Do not go overboard with pruning. Plants require enough leaves for photosynthesis so don't take too many.

Heavy pruning is normally only required once in the life of the bonsai. Once the form has been created, shaping is done with minor snipping or pinching back. This will control the new growth. Snipping will not only shape the tree, but it also causes the development of more luxurious foliage. Snip off any of the tiny spurs that grow on the trunk before they get big enough to leave scars behind from their removal.

The roots will also need pruning. Try to keep all of the fibrous roots and to keep a balance of one branch per root whenever possible. Any roots that were damaged from digging should be removed. Leave the surface roots intact. Trim the roots using sharp, sloping cuts to keep from damaging them.

Pruning will keep the shape of your bonsai and cause new growth. Some trees can handle intense pruning, but others have difficulty recovering from the trauma, particularly if they are trimmed at the wrong time of year. To prune correctly and at the correct times depends on what type you have chosen. Usually, new growth is trimmed during the growing season to maintain the shape. while pruning old season growth (hard wood) is usually done in fall.

A technique for trimming evergreen bonsai like junipers and cedars is with your fingers. This involves snipping any growth which does not maintain the desired shape of the bonsai or is too near the top. This will encourage a thicker growth and make it look more like a tree found in nature.

To accomplish this, take the growth between the thumb and forefinger of one hand while holding the branch with your other hand and pinch it off with a twisting movement. This will result in a more natural look than you would get from with scissors and also avoids the unsightly brown that scissors cause on the foliage.

For deciduous trees like the Chinese elm, maples and the cotoneaster, it is best to use scissors. Trim any shoots of outward growth, but don't cut the foliage itself.

Leaf pruning, also called defoliation in bonsai is used for many of the deciduous and tropical plants like ficus and maples to reduce leaf size, remove unaesthetic leaves and speed growth. This should be done in mid-summer. You should remove 60-90% of the leaves from the tree. Leave at least 10% of the leaves so that the tree keeps its energy.

Use sharp scissors and cut from directly behind the leaf. Over the next several weeks keep the plant in an appropriate position and climate and give it adequate water. This type of pruning is only for certain types of trees.

Choose your scaffold branches early on. These are the branches that you allow to grow and prosper, while the others will be pruned off.

Take care when choosing which branches to keep so the tree remains in balance and proportion and aesthetically pleasing. Prune the plant into a tree shape or a form that is seen in nature in keeping with the goals of bonsai.

A bonsai must be kept miniature. This involves a lot of trimming and removal of growth in the spring. Never remove all the new growth at one time or else the health of the tree will suffer. Pruning your bonsai two or three times a year is sufficient. This should be done at the beginning of spring, near the end of summer and occasionally it may need trimming in either the late fall or winter.

Once you have finished with pruning, your plant can be wired.

Wiring

Wiring is a critical component of styling bonsai, and almost every well-designed bonsai will have been wired at some point. It may be a bit intimidating for beginners to learn the technique of wiring, but it will give you the ability to manipulate the trunk and branches of your bonsai.

By coiling wire around the branches, you will be able to bend the tree into the appropriate position where it will then be held in place by the wire. Eventually the branch or trunk will learn to stay in this position even when you take the wire off. In this way, straight branches and trunks can be manipulated and young branches that are wired into a downward or horizontal position will create the illusion of age. Branches and foliage can be moved to fill in bare spots.

Wiring removes the obstacle of having to wait for shoots to sprout where you want them to grow since existing growth can be forced into position instead.

Use wire to shape the bonsai into the style that is most befitting. Carefully inspect the tree and consider its natural form and the way mature trees of this species grow in the wild. Use these observations when shaping your tree to create the impression of age and reality. You could even create a sketch of how you want your bonsai to look before you begin and then use that as a guide.

Beginners will probably do best with aluminum wire. Copper has more holding power but it is harder to manipulate than aluminum. Use a wire thickness that is a third as thick as the branch or trunk that you want to bend.

Don't water the plant the day before you intend to wire it. This lack of water will make it more flexible. Start at the bottom of the tree when wiring. First anchor your wire at the base of your plant by pushing it into the soil. Place foam pads under your wire to protect the limbs.

The technique of wiring and curving will cause multiple tiny splits and cracks under the barks surface. When it heals the new position is learned by the trunk or branch. The quicker the branch is growing during this process the quicker it will heal, and the sooner the wire can be removed without the branch going back to its previous position.

Whenever you are able to, the wire should be applied at a 45-degree angle to the direction of the branch you're wiring. Hold the beginning of the wire/anchor firmly in your left hand while you coil the wire further down the branch or trunk. The wire that has already been applied should be firmly in place and unable to move while you continue to wire the rest of the branch.

With the wire in your right hand, feed the wire through your thumb and index finger as you make a winding movement with your wrist around the branch; carefully work the rest of the way down the branch and towards yourself.

You can cut the length of wire about 1/3 longer than the branch you are wiring or you can keep the reel of wire in your hand and cut to length after you have reached the end of the branch. Always start you wire at the base of the branch and end at the tip.

The final turn of the wire should be at approximately a 90-degree angle to the direction of the branch to secure the end of the wire at the tip.

If you are working on a quick growing species you should wire more loosely to minimize the risk of the wire cutting into the trunk. When wiring a whole tree, start at the trunk, then move to the primary branches and do the secondary branches last.

Bend the branches gently. Listen and watch carefully for signs of the branch cracking. If it does, stop immediately. The thicker the branch, the greater the required force needed to bend the branch. Thick branches are less elastic than thinner branches. The branches of some species are more prone to splitting or breaking, regardless of their girth.

Learn which species are more likely to bend easily and which are more likely to break. When wiring a species that you are unsure of, test the tension of the branch with your finger before you attempt to wire.

Some species are impossible to bend without causing the branches to break. These can only be wired when the branches are very young, before they lose what little flexibility they have.

If at all possible, use your hands as a clamp to hold the outside of the branch with your fingers, push and bend the branch gently from the inside of the curve with your thumbs. This gives you more control and will spread the force of the bend around the outside of the branch where it is more likely to split.

Attempting to bend branches at the point where they grow from the trunk can be troublesome. Some species are prone to ripping completely out of the trunk. Proceed with caution.

Before you begin wiring make sure you have allowed the tree's soil to dry out a bit. With less water the branches will be more flexible. Once you have bent a branch into the desired position, leave it alone. If you try to keep moving it you risk fractures that will weaken it. Make any sharp bends at leaf joints and where the secondary branches grow because this is where tree branches will have a natural change in direction. If you make bends in the internodes it will look unnatural.

Add movement so that secondary branches are on the outside of the bend. On deciduous species, be sure to add movement to all of the straight sections on your branch. Don't just add movement from left to right. You should create up and down movements for best results.

Trees must be allowed recovery time after wiring to heal. Never attempt to wire unhealthy or weak trees or the recovery period will be much longer.

When wiring the trunk of a tree, the start of the coil is usually anchored into the soil and roots of the tree. This isn't always the best technique because the anchorage is weak and the wire can move and disturb the roots when the coil is moved around the upper area of the trunk. If movement in the first couple of inches of the trunk is not required, it is best to keep the coil of wire above the soil level.

Best Time to Wire

Due to the vast variety of tree species used for bonsai and the huge difference in climates in which readers might be wiring, it is not possible to state exactly when your tree should be wired. There are pros and cons of wiring during any season with any type of bonsai. Most species can be wired at most times of the year, but trees that are wired in the winter months might require frost protection, depending on your climate.

Wiring your tree in the winter time in a climate where temperatures drop below 15 degrees Fahrenheit is not advised and can have a negative impact on the health of your tree. Any fractures that have not healed should not be exposed to such temperatures and could lead to death of that branch.

In warmer climates, it is best to wire deciduous trees around the time the autumn leaves begin to fall. It is easier to wire and adjust the branches when they are bare since it gives you a better view of the tree. All but the largest cracks should have time to heal before the tree goes dormant for the winter months.

Deciduous trees can be wired in the spring time before the leaves open, but be very careful not to dislodge any flower buds or leaves. Deciduous and broadleaf trees can be wired at any time during their growing season, but when in leaf it is much harder to view the entire structure of the tree and wiring around the leaves can be troublesome. Branches that are wired during this growing season, especially the new shoots, will heal rapidly. On fast growing types, you should check every couple of days that the wire is not cutting in.

The next best time to wire deciduous trees is during the middle of summer after the tree is defoliated. The branches should learn their new positions and be ready for wire removal before the end of Autumn.

Because coniferous species can continue to heal during winter you can wire them at any time from spring through fall. The wire on Coniferous species will need to be left on the branches for a longer period, so frost protection will be required if the temperatures go below 15 degrees Fahrenheit.

Coniferous species will require wiring once per year, including at least one total wiring of the whole tree for a successful design. They are best wired during midsummer to early autumn.

By late midsummer, new growth will require wiring and will recover quicker than at other times of the year. Some species, for example Pines, will have made most of their yearly increase in branch thickness by late summer. Wiring after this time will allow the wire to remain on the tree until the next year without cutting in or scarring the bark.

Coniferous species can be wired in the spring and will get used to its new position quickly, but will need reapplying as new growth occurs. Any wire that has been left on the tree by the middle of summer should be checked often to avoid wire scarring; especially on Pines that swell suddenly at this time.

Tropical species can be wired any time you choose since they are protected from frost and have a short dormant period or no dormant period at all. Because tropical species tend to grow quickly, the wire should be checked frequently to avoid cutting into the bark. The wire can be removed after 6 months and the branch should be ready to stay in position on its own.

Don't try to unwind wires because you could break the branch. Use your wire cutters and carefully cut the wire away.

Water and Fertilizer

Watering may seem like a simple technique, but it is the second most common cause of problems. Too little water will kill or damage most trees. Too much water and you can end up with root rot.

Trees should be checked daily for their water needs but should only be watered as necessary. Watering too often will cause sodden compost which suffocates the roots of your tree.

The surface of the compost must be allowed to dry between watering. Only then should you water again. The time between needing additional water can be as short as 12 hours to as long as 7 days depending on factors like temperature, wind, and level of humidity.

Because of the limited amount of space in the container, bonsai care can be difficult. The shallow pots limit the expanse of the bonsai's root system and make watering practically its own art form.

Some species can survive periods of dryness, other species thrive best when kept damp. Weather conditions can promote speedy drying. Monitor the soil for dampness every day and only give water when needed. You do want the top level to dry out a bit before watering again, but you don't want the soil to be left bone dry even for a short time.

Some plants cultivated for bonsai, such as the Juniper, won't show signs of drying and damage until it is too late. It may appear green and healthy even though its root system is dead.

Bonsai should be fertilized once or twice per month during the growing season. Use a water-soluble fertilizer. For best results, apply it when the soil is damp and only use it before and during active growth. House plant fertilizer will suffice and should be diluted a quarter to a half strength.

Repotting

Most bonsai will require repotting once per year to maintain their health.

Re-potting prevents bonsai from being pot-bound and encourages the growth of new feeder roots which let the tree absorb more moisture. The soil should be replaced with fresh soil at this time.

One way to know that it's time for repotting is when water takes a long time to drain or if you see roots looking like they are too crowded around the sides of your container.

Gently lift the tree out of its current container by tilting it to one side and moving it by the base of the trunk. If it is not coming free easily try gently tapping the container. If it still will not come free easily try gently poking a stick through the bottom to push the root ball out.

Then, carefully remove any other plants or decorations. A chopstick or knitting needle is helpful for this. Be gentle with any tangles in the roots. Begin on the edge and gradually work your way around. Try to "comb" the roots gently but don't pull or tug at them so as not to cause any damage to the main roots.

Continue to gently shake and brush off the soil until you have removed approximately half of the soil from the base and edge of your root ball.

Spray the roots with a little bit of water. This will help remove the old soil and will keep them from drying out while you are pruning them.

You will need very sharp scissors or bonsai cutters to prune the roots. Make sure you have rinsed away most of the soil first. If you cut through soil your scissors will get dull very quickly.

First, cut off any old brown roots that have grown close to the edge of the container. These restrict the growth of new feeder roots and should be removed. Cut off at least a third to a half of these old roots. Be careful not to cut any new feeder roots.

Then, begin cutting the thinner roots that hang below the depth of your container. Trim them into a shape that is suitable for your container and that will leave a space of about a half inch to ¾ inch between the roots and the edge of your container.

Wash out the container or choose a new pot that suits your tree. Cover the drain holes with wire mesh. The tree will need something to anchor it so that it doesn't get blown over by the wind or tip over from being moved.

Thread some wire through the drain holes to create an anchor. Then pour in a thin layer of gravel. Top it off with a layer of fresh new soil.

Decide where you will position your tree in the pot. Likely somewhere slightly off center and towards the back. Make a small mound of soil where you are going to place your bonsai. Gently place your plant on the mound and spread its roots evenly across the soil.

When you are satisfied with the position of your tree, take the wires that you threaded though the drain holes and twist them together over the root ball until it is held firmly enough not to tip from the wind. Do not make it so tight that you damage the roots. These wires must be left in place for a few months until your tree roots settle in.

Next, add more fresh soil until you have a layer that is as high as the base of the trunk. Tap the side of the container with your hand to make sure the soil settles and fills in any gaps around the roots. Use a chopstick or other stick to integrate the roots into the soil.

Once you have finished with the soil, you can augment your design with accent plants, rocks or moss. If you are using moss, make sure you have removed its original soil before you plant it.

When you are happy with your design you should water the tree. This may cause the soil level to sink and additional soil may have to be added. Place your tree where it will not suffer any temperature extremes and out of direct sunlight where it can recover. Don't use fertilizer yet because it can burn the roots or further stress the plant. Wait about a month for the roots to recover before fertilizing. Now that you have pruned the roots you should also prune the branches.

Seasonal

Bonsai from trees in the wild must remain outside except for short periods of time when they are brought inside for viewing. This should not be for more than a few hours per day and should not occur in summer time at all unless they are placed in a well-ventilated area.

In the summer, bonsai trees require cool nights, daylight sun, and mist just about every day. If this is not your natural climate you must provide these conditions for your bonsai. Protect your tree from temperature extremes, wind, heavy rain, and too much sun light. The tree should be watered every day in the summer, but do not let it become over watered.

One of the best ways to achieve optimum drainage for your bonsai is to place it on a slat stand in your yard. The optimum placement would be where the tree can get 3 to 5 hours of direct sunlight per day with some shade in the afternoons.

In the Autumn, it is time to get your bonsai ready for winter. Watering in smaller amounts and less frequently will slow down the growth and prepare the tree for colder months. Do not trim any branches after the middle of August and stop applying fertilizer at this time.

Just as full-size trees will lose their leaves in winter, so will your bonsai. This is to be expected and they will grow back in the spring. Winter winds and freezing temperatures can kill a bonsai.

During the winter you will probably only need to water your bonsai every other day. Do not over water.

Bonsai do well outside in temperatures above freezing. Below this point, they require protection. Keeping them inside could cause them ill health so do so only if it is your only option. Even a box outside can offer protection from winter winds. You could also cover your bonsai with a tarp at night and remove it during the day.

Woody plants need a cold winter dormancy period to survive. If you do not give them this time, they won't live.

Temperate climate species have a biological clock that makes them slow their growth to survive the winter. It prepares their soft tissues for the freezing temperatures.

Some people place their bonsai in the ground for winter because the ground temperature doesn't get as cold as the air. If you choose to do this, bury the bonsai still in its container in the ground up to the rim and cover the pot with mulch or dead leaves. You can skip this step if you live in an area with a lot of snowfall since the snow will serve as insulation without needing mulch.

If your Bonsai spends the winter in the ground it will wake from dormancy when spring arrives. That is not the case with other winterization methods such as placement in an unheated cellar or garage or other outbuilding. These methods may be more convenient since there is no digging or mulching involved, but because these buildings warm very quickly in the spring, the trees will come out of dormancy and require sunlight before the temperatures outdoors are not yet ideal.

Whichever winterization method you choose, make sure the root balls are damp when the tree is put away. Check them at least once a week to make sure they aren't too dry. The placement you choose should be shaded for most of the day. The best positions are east or north facing.

When the trees begin to grow they will be able to survive brief periods of frost. Once the buds have opened and leaves begin to unfold they can suffer serious frost damage. If temperatures drop back below freezing in the spring, the trees should be sheltered until the threat of frost has passed.

When spring arrives, it is time to begin new bonsai, trim the old ones, and continue with training measures through the growing season.

Showing Off Your Bonsai

After all your hard work has paid off, you will want to display your bonsai for everyone to see. Position your bonsai so that it is at eye level with the front of the tree facing forward. Never place bonsai on the ground.

Simplicity is important. You may choose to display your bonsai alone on a stand or in a collection as you acquire more trees. Make sure your tree is placed where it can get the appropriate amount of light or shade for its needs, and where the details of the tree can be best appreciated.

A gravel bed in the garden makes a lovely background for bonsai outdoors. A simple stand or table in front of a blank wall is a good indoor setting.

Try your bonsai in various locations around your house, inside and out, to see where it looks best. A single display on a window ledge or the sunny spot on a bookshelf can make for a stunning display of elegance.

Putting a redwood or bamboo shelf unit in a room with appropriate lighting and ventilation can create an indoor garden display if you have a group of bonsai you would like to showcase.

You could turn the entry hall of your home into a beautiful walk-through of bonsai or turn your deck or patio into a lovely garden by displaying your bonsai on railings, benches or plant stands. Try to incorporate colors and textures of plants stands that compliment your bonsai as you did with its container.

Showcase them on wood, metal, stone, or whatever texture works best with your plant. Bonsai is a product of the artist and is uniquely your own.

Conclusion

Bonsai is not about perfection. You will make mistakes and that is ok.

Trees will die. This is just a fact. Especially when you are a beginner. Commit to learning why every tree dies and what you can do to prevent it. Learn from your mistakes so that you can prevent them from recurring.

When you plant a tree in a pot, you are responsible for its care. Bonsai is a responsibility, not just a hobby. If you practice it with patience and care you will be rewarded with a living piece of art.

Avoid the usual mistake beginners make of constantly trimming, fiddling with, and moving your tree. Check daily to see if your tree needs water, but otherwise just leave the tree alone.

Pruning to shape is necessary at times, but for good health the tree needs to be allowed to grow. Prune only when necessary, do not over trim just because a leaf may appear out of place.

Timing is crucial. Do not repot or prune at the wrong time of the year. Doing so can cause poor health in the tree. A tree that is repotted at the wrong time of year might not survive. If it does survive it is not likely to remain healthy.

Trees are living things. They need time to heal after one operation before the next procedure. Allow 1-3 months after wiring or replanting before you work on the tree or until you see signs of vigorous growth.

Do not fear that bonsai is too hard to learn. Do not be afraid that it is too expensive or that it will consume too much of your time.

Bonsai is fun, relaxing, and a unique living art form. It doesn't have to be expensive, but it is a commitment that requires patience and skill.

Things may not always work out the way you planned, but don't be discouraged. Even the Japanese bonsai masters were beginners once.

Bonsai can be intimidating for beginners, but it is as simple as you make it. There are a multitude of species and varieties to choose from and so many techniques to improve their appearance. There are many do's and don'ts, but the most important thing for a beginner is to simply keep your tree alive and maintain its shape.

Once you have been successful with your first tree your confidence will soar. You will be ready to learn more advanced techniques.

You might worry that you are just not able to grow a world-class bonsai. That's fine! It doesn't have to be perfect to be your own masterpiece. If it is beautiful to you, it is something you can be proud of.

Don't get discouraged or think you must adhere to strict rules. Just grow your tree and enjoy your results.

If you found this book helpful and learning about Bonsai trees, I would be forever grateful if you would leave a review on Amazon. Reviews are the best way to help your fellow Bonsai enthusiasts sort through the nonsense and find the quality books so make sure to help them out! You can leave your review HERE.

28720552R00046

Printed in Great Britain
by Amazon